100 Orchids
for
Florida

Pineapple Press, Inc.
Sarasota, Florida

Inquiries should be addressed to:

Pineapple Press, Inc.
P.O. Box 3889
Sarasota, Florida 34230

www.pineapplepress.com

Library of Congress Cataloging-in-Publication Data

Kramer, Jack,
    100 orchids for Florida / Jack Kramer. — 1st ed.
        p. cm.
    Includes index.
    ISBN-13: 978-1-56164-367-7 (pbk. : alk. paper)
    ISBN-10: 1-56164-367-X (pbk. : alk. paper)
    1. Orchid culture—Florida. 2. Orchids—Varieties—Florida. I. Title. II. Title:
One hundred orchids for Florida.
    SB409.5.U6K728 2006
    635.9'34409759—dc22

                                                    2006013067

First Edition
10 9 8 7 6 5 4 3 2 1

Design by Shé Heaton
Printed in China

Taxonomists change orchid names as research continues, so some of the names in this book may be different by the time this book goes to press.

Neither the author nor the publisher can be held responsible for any injury incurred from poisonous plants. Check with local authorities should you have any question about bringing a plant into your yard or home.

Contents

Author's Note

I have grown orchids since 1960 and through the years have written several books on these amazing plants. I wrote my first book on species orchids, *Growing Orchids at Your Windows* (Van Nostrand, 1963), a general how-to book. I also wrote *Rare Orchids You Can Grow* (Doubleday, 1968), and later, *Botanical Orchids* (Garden Art Press, 1998). In 1989 I wrote *The World Wildlife Fund Book of Orchids* (Abbeville, 1989), which was translated into four languages. More recently I published *A Passion for Orchids* (Prestel, 2002).

When I moved to Florida in 1985 I cultivated many orchids and wrote *Orchids for the South* (Taylor, 1994), which concerned growing our favorite plants in eleven Southern states. Since that time much has changed in the world of orchids, and cloning (tissue culture) has brought orchids at affordable prices into thousands of homes. It then came to mind there was no specific book on growing orchids in Florida—and thus this new book, *100 Orchids for Florida*, a guide to growing orchids in our state, where most orchids will thrive. I have attempted to present here the most current data on growing orchids in Florida. It is, as are all my books, based on personal experience with all the plants I write about.

I hope you enjoy this latest work and that it will bring pleasure and joy into your life with orchids . . . perhaps the most glamorous of all flowers.

Jack Kramer
Naples, Florida

Introduction

We live in an area blessed with a benign climate (other than, of course, hurricanes). Some people call it Paradise, the land of sunshine and warmth. And this is mostly true. We rarely have frosts in subtropical southern Florida; overall our climate throughout the state all year is never severe.

Obviously in a warm climate we can grow many tropical plants: hibiscus, plumerias, and other beautiful flowers, but none can outdo the popularity and glamour of orchids. No other plant family offers such a variation of flowers that range from the size of a pinhead to the magnificent dinner-plate-size flowers such as we see in the cattleyas. Nor is there a flower that has the decorative drama orchids bring to landscape or home.

Orchids are tough plants that can survive (if necessary) neglect and can grow and flower on their own without much care—as evidenced by the several orchids in my Naples garden. These are indeed plants that want to survive.

Basically, while orchids come from all over the world, the majority of cultivated plants are from the tropics: Central America, South America, Asia, Africa, India, Borneo, Thailand, the Philippines, and New Guinea. What do these geographical areas have in common? Tropical climate, where temperatures rarely fall below 45º F at any time of the year, a perfect world for orchid growing— similar to our climate in the southern part of the state.

Today with cloning (meristem culture) there is an array of orchids to choose from. It would take lifetimes to grow the many orchids available. Hybridization is at its peak with thousands of named orchids: cattleyas and laelias especially, and other genera as well. Now everyone can afford a few orchids in the home and enjoy the beauty of the flowers—a pleasure once only available to royalty or the very rich.

During the golden years of orchids, the eighteenth and nineteenth centuries, orchids were so desirable in England that they were not sold at nurseries but rather auctioned to the highest bidder.

People have cultivated orchids in various countries for hundreds of years, but only recently have some long-held propagation misconceptions about the plants been corrected. Though always revered for their dramatic beauty, in the past orchids were often maligned as parasites. Only recently has that old belief been debunked.

In our modern world we can all grow and feast our eyes on the beauty of orchids, and perhaps nowhere else more so than in Florida, with its mild subtropical and temperate climate.

Orchids take center stage in an atrium.

All About Orchids

Tropical Climate

Orchids grow in many parts of the world but are prevalent in the warm countries such as Malaysia, Java, Borneo, Sri Lanka, Brazil, and New Guinea. It is the amenable climate of the countries that have the insects, and even certain mammals and birds, that serve as pollinating agents for the orchids. For example, small bats pollinate the *Angraecum* orchid from Madagascar, and hummingbirds pollinate several different orchids.

New Guinea leads the world in population of orchids. There we find sharply defined wet and dry seasons—much the same as the climate in Florida, where we have our rainy summers and dry winters. Parts of South America, such as Chile, Peru, Colombia, and Ecuador, abound in orchids. Borneo, Mexico, Africa, and Florida also harbor native orchids. There are only three indigenous species in Hawaii (all inconspicuous) although it is a commercial area for orchid growing.

One of the many *Phalaenopsis* hybrids.

Let's take a peripheral scan of where certain orchids grow. Forty-six species of cattleyas are found from Costa Rica to tropical America. *Phalaenopsis* are from tropical and subtropical Asia to northeast Australia. *Phaius*, a ground orchid, mainly grows in tropical Africa and the Pacific islands, and cymbidiums thrive in tropical and subtropical Asia to Australia, with some found in Japan, where it once was the favorite flower in their art. Oncidiums are native to tropical and subtropical America. Such is the diversity of this glamorous plant family.

Many of the cultivated orchids are from tropical countries in the region between the Tropic of Cancer and the Tropic of Capricorn where rainfall is heavy, about 80–100 inches a year, which is more than Florida's average rainfall of 54 inches per year, but the timing of our rainy season is similar to that of the tropics. In Chile, Peru, Ecuador, and Colombia along the coast, and inland in Bolivia and Argentina climate varies with the seasons. The inner area of South America along the west coast can be somewhat cool at times because of the mountains. The seasonal variation in rainfall also affects the type of orchids that grow. The hottest months in the West Indies are July and August, when temperatures soar to 80–100° F, similar to Florida.

Burma, China, Thailand, India, and Indonesia have many orchid species, but climate and rainfall vary greatly in these areas. In these regions there are generally two rainy seasons. The equatorial zone, between the Tropic of Cancer and the Tropic of Capricorn, is where epiphytic and tropical orchids grow. Beyond the equatorial zone epiphytic orchids are infrequently found.

The Orchid: Its Structure and How It Grows

Orchids are flowering plants of the family Orchidaceae. They are monocotyledons, having a single seed leaf upon germination. The orchid has a diverse appearance. Whereas a rose looks like a rose, an orchid can look like a tulip, a tiny chrysanthemum, a spider, and so on. The structures of the orchid flowers and leaves are equally diverse, with the lip often an extended petal and the leaves leathery (*Brassavola*) or paper thin (*Sobralia*).

Monopodial Orchids

Some orchids are monopodial, growing in one continuous direction. The stems lengthen season after season, as though they are slowly crawling; a lateral inflorescence or aerial roots are produced from the axils of the leaves or opposite the axils. The roots become flattened and creep along any surface and adhere with great tenacity, especially in the vandas, whose roots are utilized in the rain forest as a climbing device so plants can reach the light.

Monopodial orchids occur in the tribe Vandeae, which include *Vanda, Ascocenda, Aerides, Phalaenopsis, Renanthera, Angraecum*, and *Aerangis*. The leaves are arranged in two opposite rows, the leaves of one row alternating with the other row. Leaves can be close together or far apart; most are flat and plain, although a few species produce pencil-like leaves. The inflorescence is generally a

This small *Vanda* bears dozens of small flowers. Grows easily.

panicle—a cluster of flowers close together—as in the *Rhynchostylis, Aerides*, and *Sarchochilus*, although a single inflorescence occurs in *Trichoglottis, Arachnis*, and *Vanda*. Branched panicles occur in mature *Phalaenopsis*.

Sympodial Orchids

Most orchids have an axis stem (called a rhizome), which stops growing at the end of the season; new growth is produced in the following season. The new growth starts with leaflike scales developing and true leaves arising between the scales; many intermediate forms can occur.

Rhizomes and Pseudobulbs

The rhizomes are primary stems from which the secondary stems (pseudobulbs) develop. Rhizomes can be of various shapes and small, large, long, or short, depending on the genus. In genera like *Masdevallia*, the rhizome is so short that it is almost unnoticeable. Pseudobulbs are storehouses of water and nutrients; if the plant cannot get water it uses this reservoir. The pseudobulbs vary considerably in shape: *Cattleya labiata* has bulky pseudobulbs; *C. guttata* and *C. bicolor* have spindle-shaped pseudobulbs; and in the genus *Grammatophyllum* pseudobulbs can be as big as baseball bats. Laelias and lycastes also have pronounced pseudobulbs.

In orchids with pseudobulbs and a few leaves, such as odontoglossums, the flower spike usually develops between the first pair of true leaves. Some species produce growth of varying length and thickness. The pseudobulbs last a few years after they mature. Usually flowers are produced from new pseudobulbs, but in certain genera, *Epidendrum* and *Dendrobium* for example, flowers are borne from the same pseudobulbs or stems for several successive years.

Dendrobiums come in a wide variety of flower forms. This is an example of a cluster type.

Flowers

Most flowers are borne in a lateral inflorescence, as with *Cymbidium, Oncidium, Odontoglossum, Lycaste,* and *Phaius.* Variations include flowers arising from the base or side of the pseudobulb, growing on short leaflike pseudobulb-like extensions near the base of the true pseudobulbs, or directly from the rhizome between the pseudobulbs.

Most orchids produce a terminal flower on the secondary stem, as do the cattleyas and most laelias and sobralias. On the other hand, some genera, such as *Lycaste* and *Maxillaria,* display many flowers to a plant. Genera like *Arpophyllum* bear compact spikes. *Phalaenopsis* have long and graceful curving spikes. The species in *Schomburgkia* display long flower spikes. (Note that you may find *Schomburgkia* called *Laelia* or *Myrmecophila* as they have been transferred taxonomically.)

Roots

Roots are produced from the rhizome and are cylindrical, thickened, threading, or branching, usually long, as in *Aerides*. In epiphytic orchids, the roots consist of a central axis enclosed by a covering of loose material tissue called velamen. This thin covering absorbs moisture and retains it for some time—this is why some orchids can subsist on little water if necessary. Roots of most epiphytes are pendent, but in some genera such as *Grammatophyllum* and *Catasetum*, the roots grow upright. The roots search for moisture and frequently become thick and tangled, forming a basket in which falling leaves may lodge and disintegrate, providing nutrients for the orchid.

Rhynchostylis retusa, often called a foxtail orchid, is a profuse bloomer.

Leaves

Some leaves are fleshy and hard; others are thin and textured. In most deciduous orchids the thin leaves are plaited or folded. Leaves can be broad or thin, spoon- or spatula-shaped; some, as in

Cattleyas bloom easily with good light from a window.

Rhyncholaelia digbyana, have a somewhat fuzzy coating. Many species produce grasslike leaves; other species have club-shaped or round leaves. In most deciduous orchids the margins are solid, but some orchids display saw-toothed leaves. Because leaf variation is so tremendous one cannot tell a specific orchid just from its leaf structure; flowers must be present for true identification.

Names and More Names

The popularity of orchids in the last decade or so has produced a plethora of name changes. With the advent of DNA sequencing as a taxonomic tool, many species have been moved to other genera to form natural groups of their closest relatives. For example, some epidendrums are now known as encyclias and some odontoglossums are now called rosioglossums. These name changes occur as taxonomists keep working with plants, discovering nuances in plants which, because of pollen and other sexual changes, cause plants to be moved from one genus to another.

Also to be considered in orchid names are the many new hybrids created where two or three or four species are intermarried to make a more beautiful flower or a better color or a more robust plant. There are now over 150,000 registered hybrids. The nomenclature of orchids for hybrids is

This lovely flower is a cross of four orchids.

confusing to would-be hobbyists, and in this book I have opted to primarily use generalized species names, which are common in the horticultural trade. In a few cases I have used the nothogenus (a hybrid genus) such as × *Ascocenda* (a mating of *Ascocentrum* with *Vanda*). Orchid nothogenera have not been subject to scrutiny under the International Code of Nomenclature of Cultivated Plants, and many of those in common use are invalid for various reasons. I have strived to avoid using their sometimes confusing names. Generally I have tried to place plants in their genera as they are accepted by most growers and as they appear in many supplier catalogs.

Common names are sometimes used. This simplifies things for beginners and drives professional growers crazy—who insist on absolute parentage. But common names, such as the "spider orchid" for brassias, are usually fitting; the flowers do resemble a spider. *Phalaenopsis* are generally called the "moon flower" because the flowers usually last for a period of a moon cycle. *Phalaenopsis* are also called "moth orchids" because the flowers appear like moths hovering in space. Some oncidiums are called "dancing lady" orchids because flowers move in the slightest breeze, while other oncidiums are called "golden shower" orchids because of the sprays of yellow flowers.

Growing Orchids

Orchids are easy to grow, an opinion not readily believed in Europe in the nineteenth century. But we have come a long way since then. We now know that with a few minimum requirements orchids can be grown as easily as standard house plants. And the first old wives' tale to be dispelled is that orchids are parasites. Mainly they are epiphytes or air plants and only use their host for support. In nature they grow mainly in trees (or on rocks) and derive no nourishment from the host. Rain provides them with the nutrients they need to grow. Some orchids are terrestrial, such as *Phaius* and *Spathoglottis,* and will grow in standard potting soil or in the ground. The requirements for orchids to flourish are easily understood if you remember the basics: temperature, water, light, humidity, ventilation, and type of orchid.

Temperature

If you are comfortable with the temperature in your home, so are orchids: 65 to 70º F at night and 70 to 80º F during the day will suit most orchids. And a few nights at lower temperatures or days at higher temperatures will not harm them. Also consider that some orchids, such as *Odontoglossum* and *Miltonia* and some *Paphiopedilum,* are better grown in cooler northern climates. Generally some orchids will adjust to a slight variation in temperature, but there is no sense in cultivating the cool growers when we have so many beautiful warm-growing varieties of orchids.

Orchids growing happily on a wall trellis.

Containers

The old fashioned terra cotta pot is still the best container for most orchids because moisture dries out slowly. Plastic pots generally hold water longer than clay, which in some cases can be an advantage (so you don't have to water them too often). Size of the pot also affects how much water plants need. There are also specially made slotted pots that are good because air circulates from the bottom. Pots are selected according to the size of the plant. Large plants need 5- or 6-inch pots and medium plants 4- to 5-inch pots. Small orchids need 3-inch or smaller pots. Slatted baskets of redwood or cedar are fine for orchids and available at most nurseries. Stanhopeas, gongoras, and many vandas prefer the slotted baskets because in these water runs freely through the medium and there is little chance of overwatering.

Some orchids can also be grown on a slab of tree fern or cork available at nurseries. These can be adhered to the slab with twine; do not use wire because it can injure roots on some orchids.

Potting Medium

Fir bark is the accepted medium for potting orchids and is available in sacks at nurseries, or you can use combinations of perlite, fir bark, and charcoal pieces. The American Orchid Society's *Orchids* magazine reports that it is possible to grow orchids in peanut shells, but I have never tried that and invariably stick to medium-grade fir bark.

Ventilation

Be sure orchids have ample ventilation, especially indoors. Even a small fan at a slow speed helps. Outdoor orchids usually get all the air they need.

Watering

Most people water their orchids too much; a dry orchid has a better chance of surviving than one that is sopping wet. If a pot feels light when you pick it up, the plant generally needs water. If it is heavy in your hand, wait.

Forget about the various self-watering products on the market that supply water automatically to the plant. Some are in the form of small balls, others differ in design. Do your own watering so you can observe plants personally and see if the plant is doing well by its general appearance. Leaves should be turgid and robust, not limp and pale.

Misting

High humidity is not really necessary for most orchids to flourish—this is another misconception from England, where thousands of orchids perished because of excess humidity and little ventilation. Generally 40 to 60 percent humidity is fine for most varieties.

But if you feel that your orchids need more humidity than your environment provides, you may occasionally want to mist them. There are a number of misting or spray bottles on the market that dispense water to plants, but an ordinary spray bottle works just fine. Spray the mist around the plant, not directly on it, because many orchids are susceptible to rot if too much water accumulates in the leaf axils (*Phalaenopsis* especially). Also remember that many orchids growing together will create their own humidity.

How to Pot Orchids

As a rule, orchids like to be pot-bound and continue to grow in the same pot for several years. Constant repotting can kill an orchid. It is much better to dig out some of the medium and replace it than repot the plant too often. But there comes a time when your orchid overgrows its pot and repotting the plant will be necessary. When you see plants climbing over the rim of the containers and plants that are heavily lopsided, the time has come. First, be sure all pots and shards (pot pieces) are clean, and when you remove a plant from a pot do not force it out or tug it out. This can injure roots. Instead, gently tap the outside of the pot against an old table or tap the pot with a hammer. Gradually ease the plant from the container and carefully clean away old roots and compost. You may have to break the pot, but better to break the pot than the plant.

Fill the new container one half to one third full with shards. Set the plant in place and gently fill in and around it with fresh medium, occasionally pressing it down with a blunt-edged wood stick. Work from the sides of the

Potting with Fir Bark

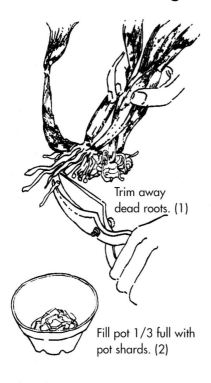

Trim away dead roots. (1)

Fill pot 1/3 full with pot shards. (2)

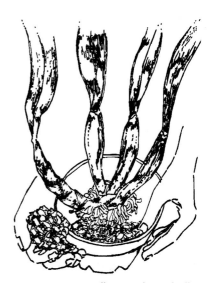

Fill around root ball with fir bark. (3)

Tamp down bark with potting stick. (4)

Tie and stake plant; label. (5)

Drawings by Andrew Addkison.

pot to the center until you have filled up to half an inch from the rim. Stake the plant upright if necessary, and on a label tag write in the name. Most orchids need tight potting. Some growers recommend the use of wet bark soaked overnight, but I have always used dry bark and it proves satisfactory.

No matter what kind of potting mix you use—and there are many, from charcoal bits to peanut shells, for example—make certain of good drainage, which is so essential to orchids. In fact, more orchids are killed by over-watering than any other error of culture. Place plants in a semi-sunny location and wait a few days before resuming watering. You can spray the immediate area around the plant and the edges of the potting medium, but never spray water directly on the plant.

Fertilizing

Feeding orchids is always a discussion among growers. Generally, orchids need little fertilizing: perhaps once every two weeks in winter and about once a week during the warm summer months. The accepted growing medium is fir bark, which is low in nitrogen, so you must supplement with some fertilizer. A 20–10–10 formula (figures indicate the percentage of nitrogen, phosphorus, and potassium) is good. There are many brands of fertilizer, but generally an all-purpose houseplant fertilizer is fine.

Most species object to heavy feeding, so fertilize with care. Too much nitrogen can prevent flowering. Try different kinds of fertilizer until you find one to which plants react well.

Winter Protection

Basically our state of Florida has agreeable temperatures all year, but of course in the northern part of the state it can be quite cold in the winter. If the temperature drops below 50° F at night for longer than a few nights, some protection is needed. Cover the plants with newspapers, cardboard boxes, or burlap (at nurseries) to shelter them from the cold. (Note: If you cover plants with plastic bags, be sure to punch a few holes in the plastic so air can circulate within the bag.) Orchids growing near house walls will have some protection against cold, as will orchids growing in trees where the foliage protects the plants.

Winds too can sometimes take a toll on orchids, but I have experienced winds here in my Naples area up to 40 miles per hour and my orchids remained generally unharmed.

Promoting Bloom

Observe your orchids periodically to see how they are faring. If the leaves of a plant start to turn yellow, check the amount of water you are giving. If the medium remains soggy, stop watering altogether for a week or so. To the eye, an orchid plant may remain dormant for several weeks: no root activity and no green leaves. Don't try to force growth with feeding under these conditions. When the plant is ready to grow, you will see signs in fresh new green shoots and white-tipped roots.

When a plant refuses to flower when it has had good culture, it may need a different amount of light. So, if an orchid refuses to respond, put it in a shadier place or brighter place to create simulated day length. I had a *Cattleya* that did not bloom for two years. I moved it to the floor away from a street lamp at night and it blossomed the same year.

If you want cut flowers, let the flowers stay on the plant for a few days before you cut them. It takes that long for flowers to mature. When you cut orchid flowers use a sterile knife.

Bug Off!

There was a time when insects in general were a plague to local plants, and orchids were no exception. But that was years ago. Today we have appropriate organic remedies and we know more about cultivating plants. Fortunately, orchids are usually without insect problems. For the most part orchid leaves—cattleyas, laelias, oncidiums, and so forth—are thick, somewhat succulent leaves and are not the usual plant insect's best dinner. There are many other plants various insects thrive on, and usually the critters seek the easily edible leaves.

At my orchid store in California I had a large ficus tree at the entrance to the greenhouse. The tree frequently drew aphids and scale and other assorted maladies, but the hundreds of orchids adjacent to the tree rarely

The author's garden room holds a profusion of plants, and orchids
bloom there throughout the year.

were attacked. Thus I used my tree as a host for the bugs . . . perhaps not a nice thing to do, but the tree was mature and generally could fight off major attacks. Occasionally a snail would attack an orchid as would a mealy bug or red spider. Since I checked my orchids daily it was easy to spot an initial invasion and get rid of it quickly.

When you notice an insect problem the first step is to isolate attacked plants so pests cannot spread through your orchids. Then apply the proper treatment. I use, when necessary, an organic remedy that contains quassia or pyrethrum. I never use a general houseplant spray or any other chemical with an oil base. This can injure an orchid.

Instead of buying expensive chemicals, I also use a solution of tobacco leaves steeped in water and applied to mealy bugs with a Q-tip®. Alcohol also works. Another good piece of ammunition for various rusts or scale is fine-grade charcoal sold in sacks at nurseries. In general my most constant orchid enemy is red spider, and for this I simply use a strong water spray, which if done diligently every week, usually thwarts red spider.

It is interesting to note that my orchid collection on trees in my yard is rarely bothered by insects. The constant air flow helps repel many pests.

Orchids Everywhere

Once orchids were confined to greenhouses and hothouses, as prescribed by growers in the nineteenth-century England. But in our south Florida climate, orchids can be grown in various places: in the home, on the porch, in a bath house, in atriums, and in the landscape. They can add glamour to almost any location.

Garden Rooms and Atriums

In Florida orchids are specially desirable in atriums and garden rooms where there is ample light and the natural elements care for their nourishment and growth. If possible, a screened atrium works well; that is where my orchids thrive, although I have constructed a roof so the enclosure can be used for other purposes as well as growing plants. I place my plants near the window areas, which are screened, so rain can enter the area and bathe the plants in natural rain water.

In such a situation orchids thrive because, unlike humans, most orchids enjoy a certain amount of humidity. And more importantly, and more like humans, orchids thrive in open spaces. A screened atrium with natural air currents is perfect if you want beautiful blooms—and who doesn't? In such a natural situation most warm-growing orchids need little help from you, though some orchid growers disagree and would recommend fertilizing. An occasional water misting with a hose attachment will keep them happy. Otherwise let nature do the work and all you need to do is admire your beautiful Florida orchids.

In your atrium you can grow orchids in various containers ranging from rafts, wooden baskets with an open slatted bottom, to standard containers such as terra cotta (which looks best) or plastic pots. Orchids can also adorn chunks of driftwood and other assorted beach pieces if properly attached. It's easy to do. Simply tie them to the wood with twine (not wire, which can hurt roots). Afford some protection from bright direct sun by placing plants strategically in an open room. Move them to places that get some sun but not full sun. Remember that in a tightly closed structure orchids will be subject to temperatures that are too high in summer, and in winter exposed to cool nights not to the liking of most of the tropical orchids we grow. Bamboo blinds, shutters, and window trellises all help to control the direct exposure to full sun.

Atrium floors can be of many materials but I prefer tile—easy to clean and not subject to insects, though possibly slippery when wet. Brick floors are also feasible, but bricks can also be slippery when wet. Gravel floors can also be used if the gravel's appearance blends with the home.

In the Landscape

Orchids as landscape plants? Why not? Several orchids such as *Phaius* and *Spathoglottis* and others are terrestrial orchids and grow directly in soil. *Arachnis,* though not terrestrial, can be grown in well-drained outdoor beds.

Planting orchids outdoors is no more problem than installing garden plants. Use standard houseplant soil and keep the plants in a semi-sunny location.

Placement is crucial when landscaping with orchids. Select locations that receive good air current. Try to have a place for only orchids, avoiding mixing them with annuals or perennials—mainly because it just doesn't look good. In most cases a lovely stand of three or four *Phaius* orchids has an elegant appearance. *Spathoglottis* are best grouped together in strategically placed areas where color is needed.

Most tropical orchids can also be grown in and on trees. As I have stressed, orchids are not parasitic and derive no nourishment from the tree, only using the branch as a host. Any tree with rough bark is a fine place for orchids, including *Aerides, Cattleya, Cycnoches*, and others. Mounting the orchid on the tree bark is simple. Select a suitable place and put a thin layer of sphagnum moss between the orchid plant and the mount. Then secure the orchid with nylon fishing line or string. Be sure the orchid is secure and does not move. Water it for the first few weeks until you see new green roots adhering to the mount and then nature will do the rest of the job for you.

Blooming orchids in trees appear like tiny jewels in the landscape and are a conversation piece. Some years ago my garden room was overcrowded with plants so I took many orchids and tossed them up into tree branches where they settled. It was actually an experiment as I used no mounting technique, but now, three years later, these orchids blossom yearly. I must admit it is startling to see the flowers when they appear because in most cases I've forgotten into which tree I so rudely tossed the plants.

A list of orchids you can grow in trees follows:

The amethyst-purple flower of the *Aerides crassifolium* blooms in summer. Half-sun exposure (three to four hours a day) is ideal.

The flower of the 24- to 40-inch *Aerides fieldingii* is usually white mottled with purple. Blooming happens at various times of the year and the orchid thrives in full sunlight.

Native to Brazil, *Bifrenaria harrisoniana* has a creamy white 3-inch flower whose yellow lip is distinctively marked with purple. The fragrant plant blooms in the spring and needs half-sun exposure.

Better known as "lady of the night," *Brassavola nodosa* can fill a garden or greenhouse with its sweet nocturnal fragrance. This native of Central and South America produces a white flower.

One of the largest of the so-called spider orchids, the yellow-and-brown-flowered *Brassia gireoudiana* is equally at home rising from a planter in a greenhouse or spiraling down from a tree. It blooms at various times of the year in full sunlight.

Cattleyas are among the most popular orchid species, and *Cattleya aclandiae* produces an intriguing khaki-shaded flower mottled with purple. It can adapt to half- or full-sun exposure, container or tree cultivation, but it is difficult to transplant once it has been established.

Pretty *Cattleya x dolosa,* with soft rosy-pink flowers, blooms in the fall and does best with half-sun exposure. The national flower of Costa Rica, where it blooms wild, is the flashier *Cattleya (Guarianthe) x guatemalensis,* which has bright rose-purple flowers and grows up to 16 inches.

Waxy white *Chysis bractescens,* a native of Central and South America, thrives in half-sun exposure and blooms in spring.

The large yellow-green flowers of the *Cycnoches chlorochilon* always impress orchid enthusiasts. Not just for show, they're also quite fragrant.

Vivid yellow flowers and easy maintenance make the *Dendrobium lindleyi* (*Dendrobium aggregatum*) a popular houseplant. It's also an excellent choice for outdoor and tree cultivation; it needs full sunlight.

The most popular orchid for the home, the *Dendrobium bigibbum* has striking white-and-lavender blooms that also make it perfect for land-scape decoration. Blooming seasons vary; the plant thrives in full sun.

Decorating with Orchids

Today many types of orchids are used as cut flowers to glamorize a home. Besides offering beauty, many orchid flowers outlast typical cut flowers such as roses, gladioli, etc.

Cut *Dendrobium* flowers are a good choice for a small bouquet.

Cutting a stem of orchids from a mature growing plant in no way injures the plant; indeed, it helps the plant conserve energy for next season's blooms. But not all orchids respond to being defrocked. Cymbidiums offer ideal cut flowers, as do the many-flowered dendrobiums and epidendrums. Oncidiums do fine in a vase of water and their branching habit makes them natural for flower arrangements.

In addition to the above orchids, flowers of the *Phalaenopsis* (the "moth orchid") are popular and add glamour to a room; indeed they are used in many stylish magazine ads. A single stem of *Phalaenopsis* in a small vase adds

A small arrangement of orchids at a flower show.

that special note of elegance. Cut your orchids as you would any other flower. Make a slant cut at the base of the stem. You can also mix other flowers, such as alstroemerias or roses, with orchids to create a glamorous bouquet.

Best Orchids for Cutting

Cymbidium

Centuries ago, Chinese painters portrayed these gorgeous flowers in their art. Two or three stems make a dramatic arrangement. You can buy the cut flowers at many florists.

Dendrobium

The reed-stemmed dendrobiums, with long sprays of white or purple flowers, are elegant and attractive. Display the flowers by themselves in a tall vase or insert them into floral arrangements for accent. Antelope-type dendrobiums—their two upright petals resemble antelopes' horns—are fine for cut flowers.

Epidendrum

These branching, spray-type orchids (including encyclias) with long stems are tiny replicas of cattleyas. The flowers, pink or brownish-pink, last about two weeks in water. To make the most effective display, exhibit one or two epidendrums in a vase, or use several as accents in large bouquets of garden flowers. *Epidendrum (Prosthechea) prismato-carpa, E. radicans,* and *E. stamfordianum* are all excellent species for cut flowers.

Oncidium

Good *Oncidium* species to use as cut flowers include *Oncidium (Trichocentrum) splendidum* and *Oncidium leucochilum.* These spray-type orchids have long stems, with dozens of flowers to a stem. The flower colors, some pink but most yellow, are beautiful when displayed singly in a vase.

Phaius

Mainly an outdoor orchid, *Phaius* bears attractive beige flowers on tall stalks. Excellent for use in a floral arrangement, the flowers last about ten days. The best *Phaius* orchids for cut flowers are *Phaius flavus, P. maculatus,* and *P. tankervilleae.*

Phalaenopsis

Phalaenopsis flowers are the orchids most often featured in home design magazines. Their graceful arching stems seem to go well with today's sleek, modern look, whether in containers or as cut flowers. Their arching sprays of white or pink butterfly-like flowers last about two weeks in water. Dozens of *Phalaenopsis* varieties (or hybrids) are suitable for cut flowers. I like the whites and pinks the best.

An orchid nursery at a commercial grower.

New Orchids from Old

Cloning

There is some disagreement amongst orchid experts about who perfected the first meristem orchid, and just when it was done. Meristemming is a process that creates a new orchid from the cells of another orchid. But there is no argument that meristem culture has reduced the price of the high-quality orchids. You can now buy an exquisite red *Cattleya* that previously might have cost hundreds of dollars for as little as $30. The meristem process allows mass production, and as the supply increases, the price goes down.

Every living plant has within it the tiny buds of new growth, a formative plant tissue made up of small cells called meristem cells. In orchid propagation a new shoot is cut off the mother plant, and several layers of leaves and tissues are peeled off until the meristem is exposed. The growing tip is then cut out (it is about a millimeter in diameter) and placed in a flask of liquid nutrient solution. The flask is then placed on a rotating wheel or vibrator, and within three to four weeks the meristem shows growth; tissue starts to develop into massy balls. In another month these clumps of tissue are cut into twenty or thirty pieces, and each one is again placed in a flask of nutrients. Within a month these, too, quadruple in size. (They can again be cut and returned to the flask for further agitation. The pieces follow the same growth pattern and can be cut again and again.) When the agitation stops, the small clumps start growing into plantlets that are then potted in seedling beds. The resulting plants are called "mericlones."

Grow Your Own

There was a time when growing your own plants from seed was a good idea. It saved money. But with the advent of tissue culture orchids available at affordable prices, the seed growing process, which takes time and patience (five to seven years to grow a mature plant), has gone out of style for most hobbyists. But propagating your own orchids by vegetative means is still a good idea because it is a simple way to increase your stock.

Vegetative propagation can be done by dividing a mature plant or taking plantlets from old plants. Both ways can produce new plants for you. To divide a plant select one with seven or eight bulbs and cut off a portion of the old plant (roots and all) and pot it up. Make the cut with a sharp, sterile knife. Cattleyas, oncidiums, and other bulbous orchids can be propagated in this manner.

Orchids such as *Angraecum* and *Phalaenopsis* form small plantlets at the base of mature plants called keikis and these can be cut and potted to make new plants. *Dendrobium* and *Phalaenopsis* sometime produce little plantlets from the stem areas that can be cut and planted to produce new orchids. Time varies for vegetative propagation, but it usually requires about three to five years to form a plant.

The cultivation of plants by vegetative means requires little care other than the usual watering, keeping the potting medium neither too wet nor too dry, and keeping the small plants in bright, non-direct light. Do not pamper the newborns. Let them grow on their own, and do not fertilize them until they are a few years old.

100 Beautiful Orchids to Grow in Florida

Aerides

These are desirable plants because they produce their springtime flowers with little care, many to a pendent stem. They are from tropical Asia and are generally overlooked. The genus carries fleshy evergreen leaves with thick roots between the axils and no pseudobulbs. The pendent spikes are axillary and bear many close-set, fragrant flowers with a waxy texture.

The plants require good watering and do well in standard fir bark potting medium or mixed charcoal. They require a bright, somewhat sunny location and enjoy a buoyant atmosphere. Allow plants to become root bound and they will produce more flowers. The *Aerides* species

Aerides odoratum - pendent spikes of small white or pink flowers, dozens to a spike. **1**

do not like to be disturbed, so repot them every three years or so and if necessary dig out old medium from the top and replace with fresh material. Provide good humidity and in the winter months allow them to dry out slightly, but never keep them bone dry as this will harm the plants. Fertilize about four times a year with a 20–10–10 plant food.

There are several outstanding species and these photographs show the ones I have had the most success with in our climate.

Aerides japonicum (Sedirea japonica) - large white flowers spotted red, many to a scape. Easy to grow. **2**

Aerides quinquevulnerum - large white flowers spotted and marked with brilliant red. Stunning. **3**

Angraecum

Angraecums can be large, miniature, or dwarf, with fan-shaped growth. The genus encompasses 200 species, mostly epiphytic, distributed throughout Africa (a few are native to Sri Lanka). The white, star-shaped flowers bloom for more than a month. Grow angraecums in coarse-grade fir or pine bark in the home or greenhouse; give them lots of bright light (but out of direct sun). They can tolerate minimum nighttime temperatures of 60° F and need good air circulation and a moist atmosphere. Repot plants only when necessary.

Angraecum compactum - typical waxy flowers with long spurs, many to a scape. **4**

Angraecum eburneum - smaller flowers than the general type but many to a stem equally spaced on wands of stems. Quite impressive. **5**

Angraecum sesquipedale – large, white, waxy, star-shaped flowers that last for days. **6**

Ascocenda

Ascocendas are hybrids between *Vanda* and *Ascocentrum*. They are so easily grown in Florida that I had to include them. They are available under too many names to list. To trace the actual parentage and come up with the name would be time-consuming. So here are three very lovely ascocendas, hybrids created by crossing the two genera to create a better plant.

At suppliers and nurseries you will find ascocendas with many fancy names and what you select depends upon your own color preference. I am partial to the rose-colored ascocendas, while other growers lean towards the orange-flowered types. In general, it is a matter of taste as to what you select, but invariably ascocendas, like vandas, will prosper in our climate.

x *Ascocenda hybrid* - a large-flowered Ascocenda hybrid with bright cerise flowers showing the Vanda influence. **7**

x *Ascocenda* hybrid - orange flowers make this plant a favorite. **8**

x *Ascocenda* hybrid - small but pretty orange-red flowers, probably from *Ascocentrum curvifolium.* **9**

Ascocentrum

This genus of epiphytic orchid has nine species native to India, Burma, and Malaysia. Sometimes called *Ascolabium,* the orchids bear spectacularly colored flowers: orange, red, and rose-purple. Spikes may have as many as thirty flowers on them and the flowers last for several weeks. Grow ascocentrums in fir bark. Keep plants very moist but never let the bark get soggy. Plants like bright light and 30% to 50% humidity.

Ascocentrum ampullaceum - flowers are rose-red, small but many to a stem, making an impressive sight. **10**

Ascocentrum curvifolium - scarlet flowers, many of them with a golden yellow lip and vertical flower spike. **11**

Brassavola

One doesn't hear much about this genus of orchids, and yet it contains one of the most delightfully scented plants I know, called "lady of the night" (*Brassavola nodosa*). Most of the species have semi-erect leaves and in general grow to 28 inches. They resent repotting so I have been more successful growing them on rafts of wood rather than in pots, where they seem to have problems initiating bloom spikes. They are not easily coaxed into bloom. The key to success is to give them a rather shady place and let them grow on their own without fertilizer, but do maintain adequate moisture.

One plant in the genus deserves special recognition. At one time called *Brassavola digbyana,* it is now renamed *Rhyncholaelia digbyana* and produces large greenish-white flowers with a fringed white lip. This species is one of the most beautiful orchids and is now crossed with other orchids to produce larger flowers. Generally they require direct sun to bloom.

Allow the medium (medium-grade fir bark) to dry out between waterings. The plants resent too much moisture. Most brassavolas will sometimes initiate bloom if nights are slightly cooler than usual, say 55° F, but otherwise they enjoy our warm humid conditions.

Here are some of my favorite brassavolas (note that two are now called *Rhyncholaelia* due to a nomenclature change).

Brassavola nodosa - I have not used many common names in this book, but this orchid is famous for its name, "lady of the night." Fragrant at night, 3-inch flowers in pure white, very handsome. **12**

Rhyncholaelia digbyana - the most sought-after *Brassavola* with large greenish flowers and beautiful fringed lip. Outstanding but difficult to bloom. Needs ample sun. **13**

Rhyncholaelia glauca - lovely three-inch whitish-green flowers, waxy and lasting. Only bears a few flowers. Difficult to grow. **14**

Brassia

Brassias, commonly called "spider orchids," have in recent years become popular because of their elongated sepals and petals, which in some cases do resemble fanciful spiders. The medium-size flowers on long stems bloom freely. Native to Brazil, Peru, Costa Rica, and Guatemala, these are large evergreen plants with leaves and bowers of blooms that are suitable for home decoration.

Once considered curiosities, spider orchids are seen frequently today and generally hybridized with *Oncidium* and *Odontoglossum* in colors of brown and yellow. A prime example of a beautiful cross is *Brassia* Rex, a superlative bloomer and very decorative.

Brassia Rex - an improved form of *Brassia* with large white flowers barred brown, many to a raceme and very handsome. Stem slightly pendent. **15**

Grow brassias with your cattleyas, but perhaps a few degrees warmer. Plants like a buoyant atmosphere and good humidity of, say, 70 to 80 percent. They enjoy good air circulation and will not do well in a stagnant atmosphere. If a *Brassia* does not do well in one location, move it around a bit until you find a spot it likes.

In general, keep brassias evenly moist all year—although they are pseudobulb plants and can get along for a month or so without much water. The plants do not need too much fertilizer; they seem to thrive on their own, but I do add a 30–10–10 plant food every three months or so.

The best brassias and those I have grown are pictured.

Brassia caudata - similar to others in the genus with elongated white petals and spotted lip. Colors variable. **16**

Brassia gireoudiana - pale green with narrow petals barred with chocolate brown, spidery appearance, hence the name "spider orchid." Slightly pendent scapes with many flowers. **17**

Brassia arcuigera (B. longissima) - similar to *B.* Rex with whitish flowers marked with brown spots on lip. **18**

Cattleya

The *Cattleya* orchid—the big corsage flower of yesteryear—has long been the favorite flower of the Orchidaceae. Today the *Cattleya* has become a popular indoor houseplant, its glamorous exotic flowers generating wide appeal. It was first brought to England in 1819 by William Cattley, a horticulturist. He sent the plants to John Lindley, a well-known botanist who gave them their name.

Widely distributed from Mexico to many South American countries, the cattleyas can tolerate a wide range of temperatures that coincide with the Florida climate, namely 55º F at night to 90º F during the day with scattered sunshine. The genus has been wildly hybridized and there are thousands of named crosses offering a treasure trove of colors ranging from yellow to pink to red to green with contrasting lips of pink or red. The genus has been so largely bred that the names read like a royal lineage. The *Cattleya* is generally bred with *Laelia, Sophronitis, Brassavola*, and other

Cattleya amethystoglossa - garlands of pinkish flowers spotted red, large, and amenable to routine conditions. **19**

orchids in the subtribe Laeliinae, so the plants are extended from their original colors of white and lavender. Thanks to breeding, there are also art-shade cattleyas in orange and pastel shades, each one prettier than the one before.

With so many mixed marriages within the subtribe to produce better flowers in color, form, and substance and also wider adaptation to temperatures, some growing problems have arisen, but generally our Florida climate suits most *Cattleya* hybrids.

The plants prefer good humidity, good air circulation, a somewhat sunny location, and minimal watering. More cattleyas are killed with too much water than with too little. I have friends who go on vacation often and leave their plants for two or three weeks without harm to the plants. Cattleyas, with their swollen pseudobulbs, can supply their own moisture if necessary. Fertilize cattleyas once a month in winter and, say, twice during summer months. Ordinary tap water is fine. Use the standard fir bark mix for a potting medium; it has been used for years and bark contains no nitrogen; fertilize as suggested with a 10–10–5 plant food. I also find that fish emulsion is a good tonic used a few times a year.

The culture for the art-shade cattleyas is generally the same as for the species and other hybrids. Although the art-shade ones produce smaller flowers than the standard cattleyas, they bear more flowers, and mature plants (five or six years old) will bloom twice a year if given proper care.

Cattleya loddigesii - whitish rather small flowers with tinges of pinkish-blue in petals. Very pretty. **20**

Cattleya harrisoniana - smallish pinkish-red flowers growing on tree branches in Brazil. Generally available now at suppliers. **21**

Cattleya intermedia - floriferous, white flowers with pink-tinged lips. **22**

Cattleya bicolor - the sepals and petals are usually a coppery brown and the lip splashed cerise, but this is a pale form. **23**

Cattleya schroderae - a fine white large flower, outstanding with butter yellow center. One of the lesser grown, but worthwhile. **24**

Cattleya (Guarianthe) x *guatemalensis* - presents bowers of flowers that are almost crimson, many to a bunch. Good form and easy to grow. **25**

Cattleya x *valentine* - rosy pink flowers sometimes spotted with tawny yellow and red lip. Very handsome. **26**

Cattleya walkeriana - rather small plant to 26 inches with large 6-inch flowers of magenta pink. **27**

Dendrobium

This is among the largest of all orchid genera with more than 1,500 species widely distributed through the world. Many are from India, Burma, and Ceylon, others from parts of China and Japan, and a great number are native to Australia and the Philippines. The species vary greatly in shape and habit but all produce beautiful flowers. They can be divided into five groups: 1) pronounced pseudobulbs; 2) evergreen cane-type pseudobulbs; 3)deciduous cane-type pseudobulbs; 4) evergreen cane-type *Phalaenopsis* hybrids; and 5) black-haired short-stemmed plants.

Any of this genus can be summered outdoors in direct sun once growth is well under way. Mealy bugs may appear on leaves of the deciduous group so inspect plants regularly.

Dendrobium pulchellum - large white flowers with purple patches at center. **28**

Dendrobium chrysotoxum - golden yellow flowers beautifully scented; generally pendent grower. **29**

Dendrobium draconis - brilliant orange centers make this white-flowered *Dendrobium* desirable. Flowers appear in clusters. **30**

Dendrobium anosmum var. *superbum* - perhaps the prettiest of the genus with long pendent stems of pink flowers on bare stems. **31**

Dendrobium amethystoglossum - unusual spreading white flowers marked with red. **32**

Dendrobium densiflorum - pale yellow flowers strikingly marked with orange-yellow. **33**

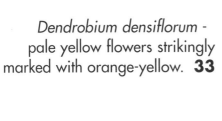

Dendrobium spectabile - greenish-white barred with purple edges, petals elongated, almost twisted. Unusual. **34**

Dendrobium bullenianum - lovely clusters of small but pretty orange flowers in bunches. Unusual but desirable. **35**

Epidendrum

For years the orchids in this genus were known as *Epidendrum*, but recently taxonomists have moved several species from *Epidendrum* to *Encyclia* and other genera (including *Prosthechea, Dinema, Oestlundia, Microepidendrum, Anacheilium, Euchile, Hormidium, Panarica, Pollardia,* and *Pseudencyclia*). The plants may be listed under both names in some catalogs. This group of orchids are a large diversified group with flowers that are usually small but profuse. I would characterize them as more pretty than glamorous.

The plants come from Mexico, Central America, and Brazil, and some species from Florida. In form they range from the reed-stemmed *Epidendrum radicans* and *Epidendrum x obrienianum* to the plants with pseudobulbs such as *Encyclia cordigera* and

Encyclia adenocaula (Epidendrum nemorale) - Two-inch flowers usually light pink or white and many to a bunch. Vertical grower, very pretty.
36

Encyclia incumbens (*Encyclia aromatica*). Over a thousand species and varieties are now grown, so taxonomy of the plants is still in process.

The pseudobulb type need a good flow of air to do their best, and the plants enjoy good humidity, say 60 to 80 percent. Temperature requirements for epidendrums are not as stringent as for other orchids. Most epidendrums

Epidendrum x *obrienianum* - one-inch flowers clustered at the top. As the lowest flowers fade, new ones appear at the top. There are many varieties, and colors range from pink to lavender to brick red. In climates mild year-round, this plant will do well outside in the garden. **37**

with pseudobulbs will tolerate 45° F for a few nights and basically grow well with daytime temperatures of 78° to 80° F. The reed-stemmed epidendrums, on the other hand require high humidity and lots of water. Coolness, say 48° to 55° F, at night will hinder growth and blooming.

The pseudobulb epidendrums like a good amount of water while growing in warm months, and a slowdown of moisture for about three weeks will force a quantity of flowers. After blooming, the plant needs a somewhat dry rest of a few weeks so it can regain its vigor.

For fool-proof orchids, albeit many with small flowers, the epidendrums are good for the beginning orchid grower. Even the non-gardener can likely be successful with these.

The reed-stemmed epidendrums without pseudobulbs are known for constant blossoming. I have had a plant of *Epidendrum* x *obrienianum* in flower for over a year; *Cattleya tigrina* (*Epidendrum elegans)* and *Epidendrum nocturnum* are also worthwhile. These require plenty of water all year and a few hours of south or west sun. Repotting is necessary every year. Average home temperatures suit them.

Encyclia bractescens - resembles
E. tampense with reddish-brown
petals and white lip. Many
flowers to a scape. **38**

Prosthechea (Encyclia)
cochleata - narrow whitish
petals and reddish centers. Very
popular because it grows with
little care. **39**

Epidendrum (Encyclia) cordigerum - three-inch purple and brownish flowers on tall scapes. As with most in this genus, easy to grow. **40**

Prosthechea (Epidendrum) prismatocarpa - typical yellow flowers reticulated with brown, small but pretty and produced in masses. **41**

Epidendrum paniculatum - bowers of whitish-green small flowers in bouquet-like style. Pretty and easy to grow. Colors may be variable. **42**

Epidendrum stamfordianum - very small brownish flowers with light pink or red lip. Many to a plant. Pendent, colors variable. **43**

Epidendrum wallisii - yellow petals and whitish lip streaked red. Unusual in the family, but desirable. **44**

Laelia

Laelia orchids are similar in size and shape to cattleyas. Most laelias originate in Mexico and are excellent choices for beginners. They range in size from very large plants that are up to 40 inches tall, to small varieties only growing to about 18 inches. Colors of flowers vary, but generally the standard *Laelia* flower is whitish-pink with dark cerise or red.

Laelia (Hadrolaelia) jongheana - spreading *Cattleya*-type flowers with sepals and petals pale pink and a yellow throat. Floriferous. **45**

The plants bear one or two fleshy leaves, and pseudobulbs vary in size; the flower spike is produced from the top of the pseudobulb. Like cattleyas, laelias like a warm climate and good humidity but will take a few cooler nights, say 65° F. Indeed, a cooler temperature at night helps force flowering. Plants should be watered all year, and while plants do not like to be dry, they can, if necessary, get along with less water than some orchids because of their pseudobulbs, which store water.

In a location with dappled sun the plants do well—neither too much sun nor too much shade is the cultural key. The plants can be grown indoors in containers with medium-grade fir bark or can also do well outside on a tree branch.

For the cover of an earlier book, *World Wildlife Fund Book of Orchids*, I used *Laelia (Hadrolaelia) tenebrosa*, a large orchid with tawny brown petals, still to me one of the most beautiful orchids—even surpassing the cattleyas, in my opinion. More laelias are finding their way into the marketplace than in former years, so when choosing orchids don't miss the laelias.

Laelia anceps var. *roeblingiana* - the crimson red splotched center is a beautiful contrast. **46**

Laelia (Hoffmannseggella) cinnabarina - a brilliant orange orchid growing in the trees in Minas Gerais, Brazil. **47**

Laelia anceps - often seen with very large pink flowers and red lip. Easy to grow and popular. **48**

Laelia hybrid - a winner with petals and sepals greenish and a vividly colored, almost violet center. Stunning colors. **49**

Laelia (Hadrolaelia) purpurata var. *flammea* - very showy delicate whitish-pink sepals and petals with wine-red splotches at the center. **50**

Laelia (Hadrolaelia) perrinii - flowers pink with variable colored lip of red or white and purple. **51**

Oncidium

Want orchids to adorn your home and garden with color and beauty? Try the oncidiums. These are a large diversified group of orchids, and while there are some cool-growing plants, most plants in the genus are warm growers, suitable for Florida's temperatures and light. While the flowers are smaller than cattleyas, the plants produce a wealth of bloom, as many as one hundred small generally brown-yellow flowers on branching scapes.

Oncidium bifolium (Oncidium caldense) - typical brown and red Oncidium flower. Easy to grow. **52**

As diversified as the family is, the oncidiums are easy to grow. Oncidiums need less light than growers once believed—dappled sunshine is fine. The temperature requirements are somewhat higher than cattleyas, namely about 58° F at night and 90° F or more during the day. Plants like humidity of 40 to 50 percent. These plants can adjust to less than optimum conditions, making them a stellar plant for people who say they can't grow anything.

The oncidiums will require more water than cattleyas; give them a good dousing of water through the summer months and semi-weekly feedings of 10–10–5. In winter less water is needed—perhaps once a week is satisfactory. Pot the plants the same way as you would cattleyas, namely when bark has disintegrated.

Oncidium (Trichocentrum) lanceanum - a real beauty with small flowers of yellow splotched with red dots and a long white lip. **53**

Tolumnia hybrid (equitant oncidiums) - miniature, generally white with red spots but many color variations. **54**

Oncidium (Cyrtochilum) macranthum - large (to three-inch) yellow flowers splotched with red center. Easy to grow. **55**

Oncidium ornithorhynchum - bunches of tiny pink and yellow flowers, many to a mature plant. **56**

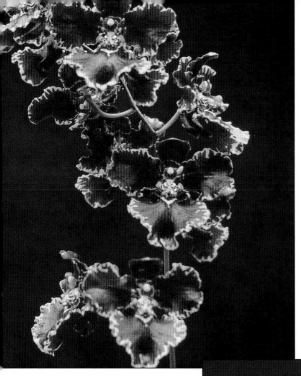

Oncidium forbesii - brilliant small red flowers lined with yellow, violet column, red spotted. A beauty that blooms freely. **57**

Oncidium (Trichocentrum) ascendens - yellow and brown and red color this fanciful small orchid. Grows in bunches; bears many flowers. **58**

Oncidium (Psychopsis) papilio - a spectacular, large (to seven inches) yellow and brown flower. Called "the butterfly orchid." **59**

Oncidium species –
a fanciful small-flowered
Oncidium I saw growing
on treetops in Brazil. It
was too high to identify,
nor could I climb the tree. **60**

Oncidium (Caucaea)
spathulata - small
flowers but plenty of
them on long scapes;
flowers chestnut-
brown barred with
yellow. **61**

Phaius

Phaius is one of the terrestrial orchids and comes from China, Madagascar, and Africa. It is a regal orchid with plaited large leaves and stands of fine flowers, many to an erect stem. The majority of varieties adapt well to varying temperatures but prefer usual warmth and humidity. While they can be grown in containers indoors they do well and make a fine display planted in the ground.

Phaius plants like some sunlight, but too much can cause leaf burn. The plants can be repotted every three years and require heavy watering and more feeding than most orchids. I use 20–10–10 every other

Phaius tankervilleae - very pretty garden orchid to grow in soil. Erect stems with four-inch flowers of white and reddish-brown to purple. **62**

watering during the growing cycle and not so much moisture the rest of the year.

After the flowers open, allow the plant to rest for, say, two to three weeks with little water so it has a chance to regain vigor. Do not mist foliage. *Phaius* are subject to pest attack, namely thrips, so use a standard household spray found at orchid nurseries. Plants are now coming to market at very affordable prices and you get a lot of flowers for the money.

Pictured here are two of my favorites that I have grown through the years.

Phaius flavus - pretty whitish-yellow flowers speckled yellow in lip; upright grower with large leaves. **63**

Phalaenopsis

Perhaps no other orchid in the Orchidaceae family has attained the popularity of the *Phalaenopsis*. With dark green spatula strap leaves and graceful wands of flowers, they are being used generously, even replacing the ubiquitous philodendrons and other green plants. Here are orchids that can bring color to any room, and whether you grow them as a hobby or use them for interior decoration, they are the leader in the orchid group for Florida. The plants are easy

Phalaenopsis amboinensis - similar to *P. lueddemanniana* but with orange-red flowers barred with red or brown stripes. **64**

to grow. After one graceful wand of flowers appears and then the top flower dies, when cut at a stem node another stem of flowers appears.

Most *Phalaenopsis* are from the Far East and a great quantity from the Philippines. They are sometimes called "moon flowers" because the blooms last longer than a full moon, but the most common name is "moth orchid" because the flowers resemble a moth. The name comes from *phalaina,* which means "moth" in Greek.

In its native habitat *Phalaenopsis* is epiphytic or sometimes grows on rocks. They prefer a somewhat shady location, making them perfect as houseplants, but without the pseudobulbs that most orchids have, they need routine watering and a humid condition. Hybridization has produced a myriad of varieties from white or yellow to candy stripe (pink and white) to cultivars such as *P.* hybrid 'Bonsall' with splotched color on white flowers.

The most famous *Phalaenopsis* is *P. amabilis.* With its many varieties, it is the cornerstone of most white orchids today. From the heritage came *P.*

Doris and subsequent hybrids such as the famous *P.* Grace Palm, a well-formed large white orchid.

For many years I cultivated *Phalaenopsis* in warmth, say 60º F at night and 80º F during the day, but lowering the nighttime temperatures in November to 56 to 58º F sometimes produces more flowers. Like most orchids, *Phalaenopsis* orchids like a buoyant atmosphere.

Phalaenopsis have no water storage bulbs, so water them carefully. Be sure water does not lodge in the center of the plant or rot can occur. Plants in small pots that dry out quickly need watering more than those in large containers. Varieties in clay pots will need moisture more than those in plastic because plastic holds water longer. In all cases, if you are unsure about water . . . under water.

Moth orchids must have a well-defined feeding program. A 30–10–10 three or four times in warm weather is satisfactory and much less during the rest of the year.

Phalaenopsis hybrid 'Candy Stripe' - one of the many decorative phalaenopsis generally called candy stripe flowers. **65**

Phalaenopsis hybrid - typical pinkish *Phalaenopsis* with fine-shaped flowers in a delicate pink shade. Very popular. **66**

Phalaenopsis hybrid - another hybrid pink-spotted moth orchid. **67**

Phalaenopsis Joshua Wheeler - probably the queen of the striped and spotted and blotched hybrids with red dots covering the flower. **68**

Phalaenopsis stuartiana - masses of small whitish-yellow flowers in bunches. Small flowers but pretty. **69**

Phalaenopsis lueddemanniana - waxy flowers with red covered with magenta bars; flowers about three inches across evenly spaced on long stems. **70**

Phalaenopsis violacea var. *bellina* - an exotic flower with yellow back-ground shaded into red. **71**

Renanthera

The epiphytic or terrestrial renantheras are native to China, the Philippines, Indonesia, New Guinea, and Southeast Asia. The flowers are red or yellow and long-lasting; they appear in the spring or summer. This genus has no pseudobulbs. The flower scape carries ten or more flowers.

The large renantheras and hybrids need full sun all day for good flower production. The dwarfs do well in a western exposure with only afternoon sun. Repot the plants every second year in bark mixed with sphagnum moss. Give these orchids lots of water throughout the growing season; decrease watering in the winter. The larger plants need nighttime temperatures above 55° F in the winter; the dwarfs do fine with nighttime winter temperatures of 55° to 64° F.

Renanthera imschootiana - brilliant red flowers on long scapes. Dramatic and does well indoors or out. Lip sometimes spotted red.
72

Renanthera storei – a very handsome plant that produces stems of brilliant red flowers, many to a scape. **73**

Rhynchostylis

Native to the Philippines and India, this genus includes four species. The flowers of these epiphytic orchids look like the tails of foxes, and thus they are often called "fox orchids." They are about one inch in diameter, fragrant and vividly colored, with about 50–100 to a scape. The fan-shaped foliage is leathery.

The fox orchids are easy to grow. Repot plants only when absolutely necessary because they hate having their roots disturbed. They need warmth, plenty of sun, and heavy watering year-round. Grow them in coarse fir bark in greenhouse conditions.

Rhynchostylis gigantea 'Alba' - the very fine member of this genus with exquisite white flowers on a pendent stem, many to a plant. Stunning.
74

Rhynchostylis coelestis - small flowers to 2 inches across, many to a scape, pendent and showy. Sometimes confused with *R. retusa.*
75

Rhynchostylis retusa - a garland of small but pretty flowers of a beautiful purple shade. Many stems to a plant. Very desirable. Showy.
76

Stanhopea

Stanhopeas hardly resemble the typical orchid we know. These plants have the unusual habit of producing spikes of flowers from the bottom of the basket. And the inflorescence has an intricate structure unusual in the orchid family. The large flowers come in lurid color combinations and only last a few days. Fragrances vary from a vanilla scent to a menthol fragrance.

Out of flower, all the species of this genus look so much alike it is difficult to distinguish one from the other. The pseudobulbs are oval, 2 to 3 inches long, and bear a single broad dark green leaf to 24 inches. The flower scape is pendent, and thus bottomless pots or rafts are necessary.

The stanhopeas like shade and enjoy a warm atmosphere and some humidity; they resent repotting, so only repot them every three years in medium-grade fir bark in slatted baskets. These are unusual-looking orchids and perhaps only for the adventurer but are certainly worth the time because of their unique flowers. Water copiously in summer, but just keep evenly moist in winter.

Stanhopea tigrina - large yellow flowers to 6 inches splotched with maroon. More bizarre than beautiful. Blooms from the bottom of the pot. **77**

Stanhopea pulla - large white and yellow flowers with brilliant red marking in the throat. Blooms from the bottom of the pot. Very showy.
78

Stanhopea wardii - probably the most popular in the genus with white flowers marked with red. Flowers bloom on short stems from the bottom of the pot. **79**

Trichopilia

Not often seen, *Trichopilia* is a genus of ideal, small, epiphytic orchids from Mexico to tropical America. These orchids bear large showy flowers on medium-size plants. *Trichopilia*'s requirements are almost the same as stanhopeas: plenty of water while growing and scanty water when resting. Give the plants a semi-sunny location.

Be vigilant about good drainage for these orchids because they will not respond in a water-soaked environment. Standard medium-grade potting mix is fine for trichopilias; be sure the plants are in an area of good circulation. Repot plants about every two years, immediately after flowering. While the trichopilias like warmth, some cool nights (when possible) encourage flowering. The flowers are large and tubular and some have twisted petals.

Trichopilia species- Pretty white flowers marked yellow in the center, with a resemblance to *T. flavus.* **80**

Trichopilia suavis - A favorite orchid with large, fragrant, and long-lasting flowers. Likes yearly repotting. **81**

Vanda

If any orchid is associated with Florida it is the *Vanda*, a plant with large open-faced flowers in an array of colors. Most are characterized by long aerial roots and tough succulent-like straight-leaved foliage. There are also cylindrical-leaved vandas called terete, but these not as easily grown as the standard *Vanda*. The original *Vanda* came from China and northern parts of Australia and New Guinea, and a few from the Himalayas in India. There are about eighty species, but thanks to the hybridization in southern Florida we now have numerous hybrids with large flowers in vivid colors. Because of its ease to grow, vandas deserve their place in Florida landscapes, especially in areas where nighttime temperatures are mild.

Vanda coerulea - the fine blue *Vanda* that has been parent to so many hybrid vandas. Somewhat pendent scapes. **82**

In addition to their beauty, vandas can be easily grown outdoors in trees or elevated locations where they are exposed to air currents and natural rain. In summer they need plenty of moisture, which is usually supplied by Florida's natural rainy season. The standard *Vanda* grows to about five feet tall. Plants have long epiphytic roots and do not like to be confined to a pot. They are best grown in baskets, on slabs of wood, or tree branches.

Plants appreciate sunlight and can tolerate more sunshine than most orchids; they can also be grown in open slatted containers available at suppliers; in this manner they receive the air they thrive on. Also available are slotted clay pots, which are satisfactory for vandas.

Although *Vanda* plants need heat—most books list night temperatures at around 60° F—the new hybrids will tolerate a nighttime temperature of 58° F if necessary without harm to the plant. Bright light is essential for heavy flowering. With *Vanda,* throw away all information about watering. These plants are greedy about water, especially in the summer months, so they thrive outdoors in Florida's heavy rainy season. During the winter they can take much less water as they rest somewhat, although some of the newer hybrids—and there are many—need more water. Your local nursery can fill you in on this information for the particular plant you choose.

While most orchids do not require much fertilizer, vandas and their cousins ascocendas will want plant feeding (with standard orchid food 20–10–10) every other watering during the growing months. Vandas

Vanda lamellata - typical of vandas, this plant bears tall sprays of small but pretty reddish-brown flowers, many to a stem. Likes sun and heat.
83

produce flowers from between leaf axils so too much moisture can cause bud rot. Water frequently but with discretion.

More than any other orchid, vandas resent being repotted. Repotting sets them back considerably, so let them grow for several years before repotting. Most vandas, if in containers, can be grown in mixed charcoal or cracked bricks or even stones.

Vanda cristata - a *Vanda* with small flowers, about 2 inches across, yellow-green and splotched magenta in center. **84**

Vanda tricolor var. *suavis* - fanciful small pink and red flowers in bunches. Pretty and easy to grow. A favorite because of easy culture. **85**

Vanda Thonglor - A hybrid producing very large pale pink and red flowers. Very impressive example of mating *V.* Jennie Hashimoto and *V.* Diane Ogawa. **86**

Vanda tricolor – Large, showy, bright red-brown flowers of incredible beauty. Fragrant. Many flowers to a stem. **87**

Vanilla

One of the species of *Vanilla, V. planifolia,* is one of the few orchids used commercially for food. The genus occurs worldwide and in tropical and subtropical areas in the Americas, Asia, New Guinea, and West Africa. The plants are vining hemi-epiphytes, with beautiful yellow flowers. The vanilla flavoring is extracted from the pods. (Vanilla can also be made synthetically.) The plant has fleshy leaves and does not bloom until it is mature (about seven years). Plants usually bloom in the summer; I have seen only a few in bloom in various conservatories.

Vanilla needs warmth and excellent sun or it will not prosper. The plant was first mentioned in Andrews' *Botanical Repository* and introduced into England about 1810.

Vanilla species – Large, yellowish-green dramatic flowers I saw growing in a tree on a beach near Cabo Frio, Brazil.
88

Vanilla planifolia - The typical *Vanilla* flower; large, bright yellow; a vining plant that takes some years to coax into bloom. This is the plant from whose pods commercial vanilla is extracted. **89**

Miniature Orchids

Most orchid genera include some very small species. These plants are wonderful for small spaces, for house plant culture, and some of them for sheer curiosity, such as *Bulbophyllum medusae* with its long trailing flowers on a two-inch plant. There is a whole world of miniatures in a book I did titled *Miniature Orchids to Grow and Show* (Norton Publishing, 1982).

Growing miniatures is no different from growing standard-size orchids. All require good humidity and air movement. Watering depends on specific plants, but keeping the growing medium just moist is suitable for most miniatures. A few need a drying-out time of about three months between waterings to force bloom.

Here are eleven miniatures I have grown through the years with success. Most of the plants here are readily available and easy to grow. With the eighty-nine orchids already covererd, these eleven minis will bring us up to. . . one hundred orchids for Florida!

Gastrochilus calceolaris – This little orchid from Malaysia and Java was brought into cultivation about 1885. Flowers are barred or striped with brown. Delightful plant with flowers hugging the rim of the pot. **90**

Phalaenopsis parishii – Variable plant in flower color but quite handsome and unusual, bearing rather large white to pink flowers. Difficult to grow but worth the time. From China and India. **91**

Aerangis fastuosa – A superb miniature with fine large white flowers. From Madagascar, introduced into cultivation in 1885. Worth every effort to find and bloom. **92**

Amesiella philippinense – Small white flowers are borne from short-leaved stems and produced in clusters of three or four. **93**

Comparettia speciosa – Lovely small plant with fine orange flowers, exotic, appealing, and desirable. Somewhat difficult to grow but can be cultivated to bloom. **94**

Helcia sanguinolenta – Flowers are showy, yellow with brown markings. Leaves short and grassy. Flowers tend to hug the pot rim. Easy to grow with warmth and bright light. **95**

Angraecum leonis – One of the smaller angraecums, but still bears the typical white flowers with short spurs. Cultivated for its winter bloom time. **96**

Maxillaria tenuifolia – Known as the coconut orchid because of its coconut fragrance. Flowers are red speckled with yellow lip. Grassy leaves. Easy to grow. **97**

Dendrobium lindleyi – A tough plant to get to bloom, but once mature and happy in a warm semi-bright place it will produce dozens of small butter-yellow flowers. Grow on a raft as it does not like pot culture. **98**

Ludisia discolor – A pretty plant, generally grown for its exquisite foliage, but also bears spikes of tiny white flowers. Likes warmth and bright light. **99**

Bulbophyllum longissimum – One of the most unusual in this group, with long hanging threads resembling a conglomeration of thready white flowers. An oddity. Blooms only in very warm conditions. **100**

More about Orchids

Commonly Asked Questions

The flowers of my cattleyas are much smaller than others I have seen. What's wrong?

Under greenhouse conditions with optimum light, flowers are generally larger than, say, plants grown in the home with less than ideal light, so few home growers will achieve cattleyas with greenhouse proportions.

Have you any general advice for getting my cattleyas to bloom? Some do and others do not.

Half a loaf is better than none. To expect 100% bloom on all plants is asking a great deal. Most cattleyas bloom better if night temperatures are somewhat cool (about 58º F). The heritage of the plant, however, may determine the way it blooms, so you might check out parentage to see if cool-growing or warm-growing parents were used and then adjust temperatures accordingly.

Some of the buds on my orchid plants shrivel and drop. What am I doing wrong?

It depends on what type orchid you are growing, but bud drop is usually caused by a sudden fluctuation in temperature. Toxic salts in the potting medium can be another cause, and not enough humidity in the air still another reason.

Some of the back bulbs on my cattleyas turn brown and die. Am I doing something wrong?

Probably not. It is common for old back bulbs to die off after several years.

Some of my cattleyas send up sheaths, but there are no buds inside. What causes this?

Many cattleyas initiate sheaths and then wait several months for buds to form. Have patience.

What are the rules for growing orchids under artificial light?

There are too many rules to list here, but basically under lights orchids need excellent air circulation, a difference in day and night temperatures, and most important, the timed light sequence must be correct. Some orchids need thirteen hours under lights, others fourteen, and so on. Consult a good book on growing plants under artificial light.

I want to grow some orchids on my windowsill. Can you suggest some easy ones for me?

I would start with *Phalaenopsis*. These plants can tolerate somewhat low light if necessary. The paphiopedilums are also good subjects for windowsill growing.

I have trouble getting oncidiums to bloom. What can I do?

Most oncidiums require excellent light, and the potting medium should never be too wet. Hybrid oncidiums with *Odontoglossum* heritage need somewhat cool nights to bloom (55° F). I would need to know the exact varieties you grow to be more helpful.

Is it true that too much plant food can result in many leaves and few flowers on some orchids?

Yes, if the plant food has high nitrogen content. Use a general plant food such as 30–10–10 or 20–10–10 a few months of the year and then switch to 10–30–20 the balance of the year.

I'm confused. What does "art shade" in cattleyas mean?

Art shades are the pastel colors such as peach, apricot, rust, and color ranges in between, as opposed to white or lavender.

What's the secret to get Phalaenopsis *to rebloom? My local florist said something about cutting spikes midway down after flowers fade on top.*

No secret! Cut the spikes above a growing node after the top flowers fade, and usually the plants will rebloom in a few months.

What do you recommend to get rid of mealybugs?

I usually use alcohol on a Q-tip®, but most growers spray with Malathion—not something I recommend for home use. Old tobacco steeped in water for a few days applied with a Q-tip® to insects also kills them.

Mildew has attacked some of my orchids. What am I doing wrong?

If night temperatures are cool (in the 50s) and humidity too high, botrytis can result in plants. Keep air moving in the growing area (a small fan works fine) and try to maintain warmer night temperatures by a few degrees.

Some of the lower leaves of my Phalaenopsis *orchids are turning limp. Can you help?*

Stop watering the plants so much and reduce humidity in the air. This may solve the problem. Occasionally, however, lower leaves of mature *Phalaenopsis* do naturally fade and die back.

My Vanda *plants just do not bloom regularly. I have some that have not bloomed in years, but their leaves haven't died.*

Vandas require very high light intensity to bloom regularly; most average homes lack this. I suggest you try some of the new *Ascocenda* hybrids. These fine plants bloom with somewhat less light and bloom twice a year in good conditions.

What is the best potting medium for orchids?

There is no perfect potting medium for orchids, and there are as many recipes for a good potting mix as there are for apple pie. Generally, fir bark is used, and most hobbyists report good plant growth in this medium. I suggest adding some charcoal chunks and perlite to the fir bark.

Should I rest cattleyas after I repot them or stick to normal watering?

I would give the plants a slight rest—a few days—before resuming normal watering, and a rest of at least a few weeks before feeding.

Glossary

Aerial roots Roots growing outside the potting mix or hanging free in air.

Anther The part of the stamen containing pollen.

Asexual Propagation by division and meristem.

Backbulb The older pseudobulbs behind the growing lead.

Bisexual Two-sexed, the flowers possessing both stamens and pistils.

Botanical Refers to species not grown for cut flowers.

Bract A leaflike sheath near the base of the flower stem.

Bulb Plant structure for storage purposes, usually underground; includes corm, rhizome, and tuber.

Bulbous Having the shape and character of a bulb.

Clone Asexually produced copy of a cultivar.

Column The central body of the orchid flower formed by the union of the stamens and pistil.

Community pot The container used for many seedlings.

Compost Decomposed vegetable matter.

Cultivar Plant form originating in cultivation.

Cutting Vegetative plant part capable of producing identical plant.

Deciduous Plants that lose leaves at maturity in certain seasons.

Dormant Resting, a period of inactivity when plants grow less or not at all.

Dorsal Pertaining to the back or outer surface.

Epiphyte A plant that grows on another plant but is not a parasite.

Family A group of related tribes and genera.

Genus A subdivision of a family, consisting of one or more species that show similar characteristics and appear to have a common ancestry. Plural is genera.

Habitat The locality in which a plant normally grows.

Hybrid The offspring resulting from the cross between two different species or hybrids.

Inflorescence The flowering part of a plant.

Intergeneric Between or among two or more genera.

Internode The part of a stem between two nodes.

Lead A new vegetative growth.

Leaflet Segment of a compound leaf.

Leafmold Decayed or decomposed leaves, useful in potting mixes.

Lip The labellum, usually quite different from the other two petals.

Meristem Vegetative propagation of plants.

Monopodial Growing only from the apex of the plant.

Natural hybrid A hybrid produced by chance in the wild.

Node A joint on a stem where a bud or leaf is attached.

Nomenclature A system of names or naming.

Offset A plantlet that may form at the base of an orchid, on the stem, pseudobulb, or inflorescence.

Parasite A plant that lives on and derives part or all of its nourishment from another plant.

Petal One of the three inner segments of an orchid flower, which is not modified to form the lip.

Pinnate Leaf form, like a feather, with sections arranged along the side of the leaf stalk.

Pistil The seed-bearing organ of a flower, consisting of the ovary, stigma, and style.

Pollen The fertilizing grains borne by the anther.

Pollination The transfer of pollen from the anther to the stigma.

Potbound Condition of a plant when a mat of roots fills the container.

Pseudobulb The thickened portion of a stem used for food and water storage, but not a true bulb.

Raceme A simple inflorescence of stalked flowers.

Rhizome A root-bearing horizontal stem, which in orchids usually lies on or just beneath the ground surface.

Rosette A cluster of leaves arranged around a short stem.

Scape A flower stalk without leaves.

Sepal One of the three outer segments of an orchid flower.

Sheath A tubular envelope protecting the developing buds.

Species An interbreeding group of plants sharing one or more common characteristics.

Stamen The male organ of a flower, bearing the pollen.

Stigma The part of the pistil that is receptive to the pollen.

Stolon Creeping horizontal stem usually producing a new plant at the tip.

Style The part of the pistil bearing the stigma.

Succulent Type of plant that stores moisture in stems or leaves.

Sympodial A form of growth in which each new shoot, arising from the rhizome of the previous growth, is a complete plant in itself.

Terete Circular in cross-section; cylindrical.

Terrestrial Growing in or on the ground.

Tuber A thickened, normally underground stem.

Umbel Flat or ball-shaped flower cluster.

Vandaceous Refers to *Vanda* genus and to plants that have a monopodium type of growth.

Virus An infectious agent that increases in living cells, causing disease.

Suppliers

The inclusion of an orchid mail order source does not constitute an endorsement for that company, nor are all orchid suppliers listed here. Addresses change and some companies go out of business, so inquire before placing an order.

United States Orchid Suppliers

Carmela Orchids
P.O. Box 277
Hakalau, HI 96710
(808) 963-6189
http://www.carmelaorchids.net/

Carter & Holmes Orchids, Inc.
629 Mendenhall Road
P.O. Box 668
Newberry, SC 29108
(803) 276-0579
http://www.carterandholmes.com/index.shtml

Fordyce Orchids
1330 Isabel Avenue
Livermore, CA 94550
(925) 600-8406
http://www.fordyceorchids.com/

H&R Nurseries
41–240 Himimanu Street
Waimanalo, HI 96795
(808) 259-9626
http://www.hrnurseries.com/

J&L Orchids
20 Sherwood Road
Easton, CT 06612
(203) 261-3772
http://www.jlorchids.com/

Krull-Smith Orchids
2815 West Ponkan Road
Apopka, FL 32703
(407) 886-4134
http://krullsmith.com/

Laurel Orchids, Inc.
17711 120th Avenue North
Jupiter Farms, FL 33478
(561) 747-9705
http://www.laurelorchids.com/

Lines Orchids
1823 Taft Highway
Signal Mountain, TN 37377
(423) 886-2111

Oak Hill Gardens
37W550 Binnie Road
P.O. Box 25
Dundee, IL 60118
(847) 428-8500
http://www.oakhillgardens.com/

Orchids by Hausermann
2N134 Addison Road
Villa Park, IL 60181-1191
(630) 543-6855
http://www.orchidsbyhausermann.com/

Owens Orchids
P.O. Box 365
Pisgah Forest, NC 28768
(828) 877-3313
http://www.owensorchids.com/

R.F. Orchids
28100 S.W. 182 Avenue
Homestead, FL 33030
(305) 245-4570
http://www.rforchids.com/

Santa Barbara Orchid Estate
1250 Orchid Drive
Santa Barbara, CA 93111
(800) 553-3387
http://www.sborchid.com/

International Orchid Suppliers

Marcel Lecoufle Orchidées
5, rue de Paris
94470 Boissy-St. Leger
France

Orchidées Vacherot & Lecoufle
BP8
F-94471 Boissy Saint Leger Cedex
France

Nurseryman's Haven
P.O. Box 51
Holumba, Kalimpong 734301
India
http://www.holumba.com

T. Orchids
77/3 Chaengwattana Road
Kak-kred Nonthaburi
Thailand
http://www.torchids.co.th/

Quick Reference Chart to Plant Size, Bloom Size, Bloom Time, and Exposure

Plant Size

Mn	(Miniature)	to 8 inches (20 cm)
S	(Small)	9 to 14 inches (23 to 36 cm)
M	(Medium)	15 to 30 inches (38 to 76 cm)
L	(Large)	31 inches and over (79 cm)

Flower Size

S	to 1 inch (3 cm)
M	2 to 3 inches (5 to 8 cm)
L	4 inches and over (10 cm)

Bloom Time

Spring	sp
Summer	s
Autumn	a
Winter	w
Various	v

Sun Exposure

Full sun	6 to 7 hours
Broken sun	4 to 6 hours
Half-sun	2 to 3 hours
Semi-shade	1 to 2 hours
Shade	light, but no sun

Note: Plant and flower size and bloom time may vary depending upon growing medium, climate, and other factors. The information given here is a general guide and is based on the author's collection grown in average day temperatures of 78° F and 10° F lower at night.

Name	Plant Size	Flower Size	Bloom Time	Sun Exposure
Aerides				
japonicum	M	S	s	half-sun
odoratum	L	S	v	full sun
quinquevulnerum	L	S	V	full sun
Angraecum				
compactum	M	S/M	a	shade
eburnean	M	M	w	half-sun
sesquipedale	M/L	L	w	semi-shade
Ascocenda	S	M	w	semi-shade
Ascocentrum				
ampullaceum	S	S	sp	sun
curvifolium	S	S	sp	half-sun
Brassavola				
Rhyncholaelia digbyana	M	L	v	full sun
Rhyncholaelia glauca	S	M	sp	half-sun
nodosa	M	M	v	full sun
Brassia				
arcuigera	M	L	s	full sun
caudata	M	L	v	full sun

Name	Plant Size	Flower Size	Bloom Time	Sun Exposure
gireoudiana	M	L	v	full sun
Rex	M	L	sp	half-sun
Cattleya				
amethystoglossa	M	M	v	half-sun
bicolor	M	M	v	half-sun
guatemalensis	M	S	v	half-sun
harrisoniana	M	M	v	half-sun
intermedia	M	M	v	half-sun
loddigesii	S	M	v	half-sun
schroderae	S	M	s	half-sun
walkeriana	M	L	w	half-sun
Dendrobium				
amethystoglossom	M	S	v	half-sun
anosmum var. *superbum*	L	M	sp	full sun
bullenianum	M	S	sp	full sun
chrysotoxum	M	S	sp	full sun
densiflorum	M	S	sp	full sun
draconis	S	S	sp	full sun
pulchellum	M	M	sp	full sun
spectabile	M	S	v	half-sun
Epidendrum (***Encyclia,*** etc.)				
bractescens	S	S	sp	half-sun
cordigerum	M	M	sp	full sun
cochleatum	S	S	v	full sun
nemorale	S	M	w	full sun
x *obrienianum*	M	S	v	half sun

Name	Plant Size	Flower Size	Bloom Time	Sun Exposure
paniculatum	M	S	v	half-sun
prismatocarpum	M	M	s	full sun
stamfordianum	M	S	sp	half-sun
wallisii	S	S	sp	half-fun

Name	Plant Size	Flower Size	Bloom Time	Sun Exposure
Laelia				
anceps	M	L	s	half-sun
cinnabarina	M	M	s	half-sun
jongheana	M	S	v	half-sun
perrinii	M	L	v	half-sun
purpurata	L	L	s	half-sun
Oncidium				
ascendens	S	S	s	half-sun
bifolium	S	S	s	half-sun
forbesii	S	S	s	full sun
lanceanum	M	S	s	half-sun
ornithorhynchum	M	S	a, w	half-sun
papilio	S	M	w	half-sun
spathulata	M	M	w	half-sun
Tolumnia hybrid	S	S	sp	half-sun
Phaius				
tankervilleae	M/L	L	s	broken sun
flavus	M/L	M	sp	broken sun
Phalaenopsis				
amboinensis	M	M	w	semi-shade
'Candy Stripe'	M	M	w	semi-shade
Joshua Wheeler	M	L	w	semi-shade
lueddimanniana	S	M	w	semi-shade

	Plant Size	Flower Size	Bloom Time	Sun Exposure
stuartiana	M	M	sp	broken sun
violacea var. bellina	M	M	v	broken sun

Name	Plant Size	Flower Size	Bloom Time	Sun Exposure
Renanthera				
imschootiana	M	M	s	half-sun
storei	S	S	s	semi-shade
Rhynchostylis				
coelestis	M	S	s	sun
gigantea	M	M	s	half sun
retusa	M	M	s	half sun
Stanhopea				
pulla	S	S	v	half-sun
tigrina	L	L	s	sun
wardii	L	L	s	sun
Trichopilia				
suavis	S	L	sp	semi-shade
hybrid	S	L	s	semi-shade
Vanda				
coerulea	S	M	w	semi-shade
cristata	S	M	a, w	full sun
lamellata	S	M	w	full sun
Thonglor	L	M	w	full sun
tricolor	L	M	w	half sun
tricolor var. *suavis*	L	M	w	half-sun
Vanilla				
planifolia	L	L	s	broken sun

MINIATURES

Name	Plant Size	Flower Size	Bloom Time	Sun Exposure
Gastrochilus calceolaris	Mn	S	sp	half-sun
Phalaenopsis parishii	Mn	M	s	half-sun
Aerangis fastuosa	Mn	M	v	half-sun
Amesiella philippinense	Mn	S	v	broken sun
Comparettia speciosa	Mn	L	sp	broken sun
Bulbophyllum longissimum	Mn	S	sp	semi-shade/shade
Ludisia discolor	Mn	S	w	shade
Angraecum leonis	Mn	M	w	shade
Maxillaria tenuifolia	Mn	M	w	semi-shade
Helcia sanguinolenta	Mn	M	sp	half-sun
Dendrobium lindleyi	Mn	S	sp	half-sun

Epilogue

Conservation

Today, conservation of our native trees and plants is very much in the news. It was not always this way. Years ago people freely collected any orchids they found growing. Now we have laws to protect endangered plants, but of course enforcing them is another issue. In Florida we have become aware of our natural treasures and have made great strides in protecting our native orchids with stringent laws. Again enforcing them is not easy, particularly in remote areas such as the Everglades. Other states have also passed laws prohibiting the harvesting/removal (theft) of orchids. And now we have CITES (the Convention on International Trade in Endangered Species of Wild Fauna and Flora), an agreement to regulate the international trade in specimens and derivatives (parts) of wild animals and plants listed as endangered. The purpose of this treaty is to ensure that trade does not threaten their survival and may help to preserve rare and endangered orchids. Although a few orchid species have been threatened by over collecting, the primary cause of their demise is habitat destruction.

I might add for any would-be orchid thieves, in addition to risking severe penalties, you will probably not succeed in growing any orchid you collect. It is truly difficult to gather these plants from their natural environment and try to grow them in your own garden. Years ago when few laws existed I gathered a few, and I can verify that cultivating them rarely succeeds. Also now, due to seed propagation and tissue culture (cloning) there is really no reason to plunder foreign native habitats for orchids. We have perfected the tissue culture procedure to grow plants—thousands of them—from one plant. This also produces plants adapted to greenhouse culture and reduces the price of orchids to the consumer. Fortunately, most of the mail-order orchid growers and suppliers saw this problem coming and, through the horticultural propagation of wild species that were brought into the United States years ago, have prevented any shortage of orchid species. Also these line-breed species are improved forms that are highly desired by hobbyists.

We all now realize how valuable and dear our plants in the wild are, thanks to the dedication and care of members of the environmental movement. Orchids, especially, are being destroyed brutally in the world's rain forests by farming and logging. Habitat destruction continues to kill off orchids in other parts of the world as well. Indeed, the decimation of orchids has been so intense, CITES has put all orchids on the endangered or threatened lists. Thus, do not try to bring in any orchids from lands you have traveled to without the proper permits. If you do not care about the orchids, care about your pocketbook. The fine for importing orchids without permits is extremely stiff.

Although the movement of orchid species is regulated by CITES, artificially propagated specimens of hybrids of the genera *Cymbidium, Dendrobium, Phalaenopsis,* and *Vanda* are not subject to the provisions of the Convention. Commercial products such as vanilla are also exempt.

It is beneficial to join the American Orchid Society. Annual fees entitle you to their magazine *Orchids,* which contains much valuable orchid information.

The orchids in our homes and gardens are gifts from nature. Take care of them, keeping them safe and healthy for our enjoyment and the enjoyment of others after us.

Photo Credits

(Photos not listed here are by the author.)

Andrew Addkison
47 *bottom*, 56 *bottom*, 79, 89 *bottom*

Beall
61 *top*

Hausermann
1, 2, 8, 73, 74 *top*, 74 *bottom*, 75 *top*, 76, 77

Marsh
61 *bottom*, 69 *top*, 91

Oak Hill Gardens
11, 32, 33 *top*, 33 *bottom*, 35 *bottom*, 38, 51 *top*, 51 *bottom*, 58 *bottom*, 66 *bottom*, 75 *bottom*, 81 *top*, 82, 89 *top*

Steve C.
5, 45, 46 *bottom*, 48 *bottom*, 63 *top*, 72

J. Wilson
48 *top*, 49

Front Cover
Top: Oak Hill Gardens *Bottom Left:* Jack Kramer *Bottom Right:* Jack Kramer

Back Cover
Clockwise from top right:
Andrew Addkison, Jack Kramer, Hausermann, Steve C., Jack Kramer, Oak Hill Gardens, Jack Kramer, Jack Kramer, Oak Hill Gardens, Jack Kramer

Notes

Notes

Index

Photos indicated with **boldface**.

Here are some other books from Pineapple Press on related topics. For a complete catalog, write to Pineapple Press, P.O. Box 3889, Sarasota, Florida 34230-3889, or call (800) 746-3275. Or visit our website at www.pineapplepress.com.

The Art of South Florida Gardening by Harold Songdahl and Coralee Leon. Gardening advice specifically written for the unique conditions of south Florida. This practical, comprehensive guide, written with humor and know-how, will teach you how to outsmart the soil, protect against pests and weather, and select the right trees and shrubs for Florida's climate. (pb)

Florida's Best Fruiting Plants by Charles R. Boning. A comprehensive guide to fruit-bearing plants that thrive in the Florida environment. Discusses exotics and native species, familiar plants and dozens of rare and obscure plants. (pb)

Groundcovers for the South by Marie Harrison. Presents a variety of plants that can serve as groundcovers in the American South. Each entry gives detailed information on ideal growing conditions, plant care, and different selections within each species. Color photographs and line drawings make identification easy. (pb)

Southern Gardening: An Environmentally Sensitive Approach by Marie Harrison. A comprehensive guide to beautiful, environmentally conscious yards and gardens. Suggests useful groundcovers and easy-care, adaptable trees, shrubs, perennials, and annuals. (pb)

Gardening in the Coastal South by Marie Harrison. A Master Gardener discusses coastal gardening considerations such as salt tolerance; environmental issues such as pesticide use, beneficial insects, and exotic invasives; and specific issues such as gardening for butterflies and birds. Color photos and charming pen-and-ink illustrations round out the text. (pb)

Flowering Trees of Florida by Mark Stebbins. Written for both the seasoned arborist and the weekend gardener alike, this comprehensive guide offers 74 outstanding tropical flowering trees that will grow in Florida's subtropical climate. Full-color photos throughout. (pb)

Landscaping in Florida by Mac Perry. A photo idea book packed with irresistible ideas for inviting entryways, patios, pools, walkways, and more. Over 200 photos and eight pages of color photos. (pb)

Ornamental Tropical Shrubs by Amanda Jarrett. Stunning color photos and full information profile for 83 shrubs. (hb & pb)

The Trees of Florida by Gil Nelson. The first comprehensive guide to Florida's amazing variety of tree species, this book serves as both a reference and a field guide. (hb & pb)